a man of vision

ST ALPHONSUS LIGUORI

1696-1787

A Redemptorist Publication

Published by
Redemptorist Publications
Alphonsus House Chawton Alton Hampshire GU34 3HQ

Text: Fr A Foy, C.Ss.R.
Design: Roger Smith

Photography: Cover, Superstock. Page 4, Zefa.
              Pages 20 & 34, Image Bank.

First Published April 1996

ISBN 0 85231 157 5

Printed in Britain by Bourne Press Limited Bournemouth BH1 4QA

St Alphonsus Liguori

Part One
The Early Years

Alphonsus Liguori was born on September 27, 1696, at Marianella, a few miles from Naples. He was the first child of Giuseppe and Anna Liguori. Both his parents were of noble lineage, counting among their ancestors high ranking soldiers and administrators in the Kingdom of Naples. Anna's brother, Emilio Cavalieri, had recently been made Bishop of Troia at the age of 30 – making him the youngest Bishop in Christendom.

Giuseppe Liguori had entered the Navy at an early age and was now an officer in the galleys. He would soon reach the rank of Captain, and finally Commander. He already had great ambitions for his eldest son, with a view to bringing more glory to the Liguori name. A distinguished career in the army, perhaps, a diplomat, or a lawyer making enough money to win the hand of a princess. Nothing would be spared on his education to ensure Alphonsus could take his place in high society as a gentleman with all the required accomplishments. In those days it was the parents who made all the important decisions for their children. And eldest sons especially were expected to abide by the arrangements made by their fathers, as they would be heirs to all the family possessions.

The Kingdom of Naples

Alphonsus spent the whole of his life in the Kingdom of Naples. That was the largest of the ten states in Italy at that time. It comprised the whole of Southern Italy together with Sicily. Its 3,300,000 inhabitants accounted for a quarter of Italy's total population. Over the centuries the Kingdom of Naples had many conquerors, including Greeks, Romans, Arabs, Normans, Germans, French and Spanish. This had left the Kingdom with a rich culture and a lively people who had grown impervious to a change of rulers – provided they did not interfere with their easy-going way of life.

Naples itself was the most populated capital in Europe after London and Paris. During the lifetime of Alphonsus it grew to 442,000. It was a colourful, musical and noisy city. Its streets were alive with five groups of citizens – the high-living and idle nobility, well-heeled clergy, a middle class, small shopkeepers who filled the ground floors of private mansions, and 30,000 beggars who slept in doorways and on public benches.

There was a sixth group made up of Black, Oriental and Moorish slaves. These were to be found in all the great ports. The 18th century was the most slave-oriented period of modern times. Navies used slaves to man their galleys. Each galley required 400 oarsmen. Besides the slaves the galleys were manned by convicts and prisoners of war, many of them in chains. Such were the crews under the command of Captain Liguori. Such a man would not easily bear contradiction. Alphonsus had a stern father to deal with, but one who loved him dearly.

St. Francis Geronimo

As far as the slaves, beggars and prostitutes of Naples were concerned, they had an ardent friend and apostle in a Jesuit priest, Fr. Francis Geronimo, who devoted his life to their welfare. He was popular with them all and greatly loved. Giuseppe Liguori knew him well and counted him among his most valued friends. It was no accident, therefore, when this holy Jesuit called at the Liguori's home to congratulate the parents of Alphonsus, and to bless their new-born infant. Taking him into his arms, the Jesuit priest made this prophecy: "This child will render great service to the Church. He will become a Bishop, and he will live to be over 90." By a strange coincidence, Alphonsus Liguori and Francis Geronimo were both canonised on the same day, May 26, 1839.

Early Education

The early education of Alphonsus fell naturally to his mother, especially as Giuseppe was away at sea for months at a time. Alphonsus was not the only child to be instructed. During the first ten years of their marriage Anna and Giuseppe Liguori had eight children – four boys and four girls. Three of the boys became priests, and two of the girls nuns. Anna was well-qualified to lay the foundations for their spiritual lives. She herself had spent ten years of her childhood in a convent – this was quite normal among rich families. Besides teaching the children their prayers she shared with them her personal devotions, above all, her intense love for Jesus and Mary. When Alphonsus was old enough for confession Anna chose her cousin, Thomas Pagano, to be his confessor; and for thirty years he continued to be the friend and guide of the future saint.

The Oratorians

Fr. Pagano was the new leader of the Oratorian Fathers. He had succeeded his uncle, Fr. Gizzio, a famous preacher, who was also related to Anna Liguori. The Oratorians, founded a century earlier by St. Philip Neri, were one of several Religious Orders leading strict lives and working zealously for the salvation of souls. St. Philip's special characteristic was cheerfulness and joy in the spiritual life. He also believed in culture and learning, and the use of all the arts to the glory of God. It was this spirit that attracted the future Cardinal Newman, with the result that he established the first Oratory in England in 1849.

The Oratorians took a special interest in the training of young people. This involved not only spiritual guidance but a programme of social activities that appealed to the young. At the age of nine Alphonsus joined the Confraternity of Young Noblemen, and for the next ten years he was deeply involved in all its activities. In particular he enjoyed the regular Sunday routine of Mass, sung Vespers, talks and readings, followed by games in a beautiful park overlooking the Bay of Naples. The day concluded with a musical concert in the best tradition of the Oratorians. From them we get the word 'oratorio' – a work of sacred music.

Early Studies

It was not unusual for sons of nobles to have private tutors. For Alphonsus, Giuseppe chose a scholarly and saintly priest, Fr. Domenico Buonaccia. It was the custom for tutors to become part of the household, and for priests to say Mass in the family chapel. Fr. Domenico remained with the Liguori family for about twelve years, so Alphonsus had the benefit of his company until he was nineteen. Alphonsus was a very apt scholar and made rapid progress in the subjects generally taught in those days. These would include Latin and Greek, Geography, Mathematics, Literature, French, Poetry, Art and Architecture. To supplement this, Alphonsus had lessons from the leading exponents of Art, Painting and Music. By the age of twelve he was playing the harpsichord with the virtuosity of a professional, and indeed, he had made such progress in his studies that he was admitted at twelve years as a student in the University of Naples.

University

Having decided that Alphonsus was not cut out for a military career, Giuseppe began thinking of his eldest son as a magistrate or judge, or possibly as an administrator with high office in the State. This would be in line with many of his ancestors on both sides of the family. For such a career a good degree in Law would be essential. So for five years Alphonsus studied civil law and canon law – the ecclesiastical law which applied to everything even remotely connected with the Church.

The power still wielded by the Church in Catholic countries, especially in the field of law, was increasingly resented by the State and by lawyers. This led to fierce anti clericalism and hostility to Rome, and to the Pope in particular. One of Alphonsus Liguori's professors published a dissertation entitled: "The Roman Pontiff has no Rights over the Kingdom of Naples". That sounds like an echo of one of the Thirty Nine Articles in the Anglican Prayer Book: "The Bishop of Rome hath no jurisdiction in this Realm of England". The Popes – and especially Pope Boniface VIII – had indeed gone too far in claiming jurisdiction over the Temporal Power of the State in the Middle Ages; and this was the inevitable and overdue backlash. Alphonsus was to suffer from it later on when he tried to have his Congregation recognised in the Kingdom of Naples. At least as a student at University he came to understand the reasons for the anti clerical spirit of the Neapolitan Government.

During his years at University, Alphonsus kept up all his

exercises of piety – daily Mass, family prayer, and Sunday meetings with his Confraternity. The only relaxation he allowed himself was a game of cards with his next door neighbours. Playing cards was an obsession with Neapolitans from the highest to the lowest, and money was usually at stake. Alphonsus was allowed only one hour for cards. One evening he was a few minutes late returning home. He found his father in a rage. All his books had been removed and replaced with packs of cards. It was a lesson he never forgot.

By the age of sixteen Alphonsus had completed his studies and passed his final public examinations with first class honours. In a glittering ceremony he received his degree and his lawyer's robe. For ten years he was active in the courts of Naples, and built up a reputation that must have filled his father's heart with pride.

Civic Duties

Even outside the courts the young lawyer had ample opportunity to learn the realities of life, and to deal with its problems. The Liguori family was one of the eighteen noble families with a right to sit on the local Council. At the age of fourteen, Alphonsus, suitably dressed for the occasion, was presented to the other patrician families and took his seat. For the next thirteen years he was involved with the business of the municipality – leasing property, up-dating city registers, collecting and distributing funds for impoverished noblemen, maintaining streets, squares and public buildings, providing police, and organising celebrations and ceremonies. As a nobleman he knew his duties and carried them out with distinction. His personal spiritual life, far from being a hindrance, inspired him to give dedicated service to his fellow citizens.

Lawyer

Knowing at least some of the dangers and pitfalls of the legal profession, Alphonsus drew up a list of rules that would ensure his integrity and honesty, and at the same time protect his clients from undue expense. His strict adherence to these principles did him no harm. He successfully defended difficult cases; and as his reputation soared he was increasingly in demand by the most influential families. By the age of twenty-one he was a public prosecutor in the courts and the kingdom, and elected as judge to decide all contested cases in the municipal court of San Lorenzo. In this capacity he had to deal with such matters as the smuggling of salt, tobacco, chocolate, and other goods passing through the port of Naples. There were also cases concerning the supply of bread and the allocation of bakeries for the entire city. Without a doubt he was the rising star of Naples.

A Case Lost

Litigation over property was nothing new in Naples. But in this case the contestants were among the highest and most influential families in the land – the Medici and the Orsini. Arguments over the ownership of a tract of land called Amatrice had been going on for years, and a great deal of money was at stake. The Orsini claimed that this money was owing to them since the property had been taken from them by juridical trickery and the machinations of the Department of Revenue in 1693. They chose Alphonsus to defend their case – a tribute to the high esteem in which he was held.

Unfortunately, but not surprisingly, corruption, bribery and political pressure entered into the case. As a result the judges set aside the arguments of Alphonsus, and accepted as valid the transactions of the Department of Revenue, and the terms which were in question. Alphonsus therefore lost this important case. The defeat was all the more bitter as he had never lost a case before. Totally disillusioned by the whiff of corruption and by the injustice of the verdict, he returned home and locked himself in his room for three days. He came out only when he could no longer resist his mother's tears. This experience ended his legal career, but opened a door which would lead eventually to his true vocation – the priesthood.

For some time now, the thought of the priesthood had been in his mind at least subconsciously. However he had not yet come to the point of a real decision. He knew how much such a decision would upset his father. Yet he had little appetite for the law courts, and even less for the empty social rounds in which he had to take part. As for any matrimonial alliance his father wished to arrange for him, his attitude was entirely negative and uncooperative. And now, having come face to face with corruption in the legal system he decided the profession of law was no longer for him, and to continue in it might endanger the salvation of his soul. In his desolation he turned increasingly to prayer and to the consolations of a deeply spiritual life.

Predictably, Giuseppe Liguori fumed and raged, cajoled and threatened, but to no avail. Alphonsus refused to take on clients or to accept cases – even one on behalf of his father. The crunch came when he refused to go with his father to a celebration in honour of the Empress Isabella. In a rage Giuseppe rode furiously to his country house in Marianella to give full vent to his bitterness.

Alphonsus, for his part, went to visit the sick in the Hospital for Incurables. It was there that the grace of God finally struck. Alphonsus found himself surrounded by a great light, and in his heart he heard the words: "Leave the world and give yourself to me." "My God," said Alphonsus, "I have resisted your grace for too long. Here I am. Do what you will with me." He hurried from the hospital to his favourite church, Our Lady of Ransom. There he knelt before the statue of Our Lady and dedicated his whole life to the service of Jesus and Mary. He surrendered to them all his titles, properties and wealth. The sacrifice was complete. As a final gesture to confirm his dedication he placed his sword on Our Lady's altar.

From the church Alphonsus hastened to the house of the Oratorians to see his confessor, Father Pagano. "I have given my life totally to God," he said, "and I wish to become a priest in your Community." Father Pagano was not entirely surprised, but he played for time. "You must give me a year to think about it," he said. Alphonsus could not accept that, but Pagano pointed out that he must try to get his father's agreement, and that would take time. It would not be easy.

Days of tension followed in the Liguori household. Things came to a head when Alphonsus finally told his father he had decided to become a priest. The inevitable storm broke around him. It was as though nearby Vesuvius had erupted. Captain Liguori could be a very angry man. But when he eventually calmed down he contacted relatives and friends, priests and bishops, begging them to use all their influence to make Alphonsus change his mind. To all of them Alphonsus gave the same reply: "I am persuaded that God wants me to enter into the service of the Church. I must follow God's call and not my father's wishes."

In the end Giuseppe had to accept that his eldest son was now going to be a priest. The only concession was that Alphonsus would be a diocesan priest and not an Oratorian. Together they went to see Cardinal Pignatelli, the Archbishop of Naples, who knew the family well. He was genuinely surprised when he heard the news. "What! Your son wants to be a priest!" "Yes" replied the father, "and I wish to God it were not so, your Eminence, but that is what he has decided." Alphonsus was twenty-seven when he exchanged his secular dress for the simple cassock of the Neapolitan clergy.

Seminarian

Although Giuseppe had insisted that Alphonsus should remain at home, he could not bear the sight of his son in a cassock. The tension in the home was unbearable, and as far as possible they kept out of each other's way. Anna was caught in the middle. She accepted that it was the will of God that Alphonsus should become a priest. At the same time she had to sympathise with her husband and try to mollify him.

Under the circumstances, Alphonsus must have been happy to leave the house each morning to attend lectures at the seminary. On his way there he stopped for Mass at the church of the Oratorians. He applied himself vigorously to his studies, and took part in lively academic discussions.

He read widely in Theology, especially the works of St. Thomas

Aquinas, the writings of the early Fathers, and the history of the Church. His favourite book, of course, was the holy Bible which he read every day, making it the subject of his meditations. While he appreciated the importance of a thorough academic training, he kept in mind the pastoral needs of ordinary people and especially the poor.

The Confraternity of Doctors

As a seminarian Alphonsus kept up not only his devotions but also his works of charity. At the age of 19 he had joined the Confraternity of Doctors which was open to noblemen with university degrees. Among their duties was to care for the sick in the largest hospital of Naples which took in 1,300 cases of physical and mental suffering. The dregs of humanity found a place there, but without hygiene they rotted away in filthy and contagious conditions. The Confraternity of Doctors financed 48 beds with its alms, and cared for 310 sick people. The Doctors made their beds, consoled them and fed them. There was a rota of service on weekdays, and all worked together on Sundays. These young knights saw and served Christ in the poor and the wretched.

The Misericordia

The Liguori family were involved with another Confraternity called the Misericordia (Mercy). Among their duties was the burial of poor people who could not afford a proper funeral. Dressed in white albs and red capes at least thirty of them accompanied the procession to the place of burial singing psalms. They also maintained a hostel providing free lodgings and meals for pilgrims and foreign priests. Next to the hostel was a hospital where they cared for priests who had no money. To pay for their good works the knights had to beg in the city dressed in their albs and capes – and this was a hard test for their pride. Some of the money they collected was used to bring comfort and good meals to priests languishing in diocesan jails. These varied experiences over a period of ten years taught Alphonsus many lessons and helped to prepare him for the priesthood and for the work that lay ahead.

Apostolic Missions

Besides following the seminary programme of prayer and study, the day students were assigned as helpers to different parishes. One of their duties was to catechise the children. They also had to attend the weekly meetings of one of three ecclesiastical associations. Alphonsus chose the Apostolic Missions, a group of priests and brothers who developed their own spirituality through conferences and discussions, and gave regular parish Missions. This training was to be of vital importance to the future Founder of the Redemptorists. In this work Alphonsus found himself in his true element, and threw himself into it with great enthusiasm.

The first mission in which he played a part was in the most notorious area of Naples, where thieves, prostitutes and riff-raff abounded – definitely a no-go area for the rich and refined. Through narrow streets, swarming with merchants, artisans and ragged urchins, Alphonsus and his companions made their way in procession, singing hymns, carrying a cross, and ringing a bell to attract a crowd. At various points they stopped to urge everyone to attend the mission. Other groups were leading processions and gathering crowds from other directions. When they all eventually converged on the church they had more than enough people to fill it. Then before the Blessed Sacrament the opening sermon would be preached. A team of forty priests took part in the mission which lasted for two weeks. Alphonsus played a useful part leading the singing, collecting the crowds and dealing with the children. His skill as a lawyer was also put to good use in reconciling bitter enemies, and drawing up legal documents putting an end to long-standing vendettas. As soon as the mission was over the students returned to their studies.

The White Brethren

During his seminary years, Alphonsus found wider scope for his charity in ministering to those condemned to death. In 1725 he joined the Confraternity of White Brethren – so named because of the habit they wore as they accompanied prisoners to execution. For several days before the execution members of the Confraternity

– mostly priests – gave spiritual comfort and assistance to the condemned. On the day of execution at least thirteen members led the procession, chanting the penitential psalms and praying with the prisoner. Prisoners belonging to the upper class were beheaded, other citizens were hanged. After the execution the Brethren took the body to their own chapel, recited the Office for the Dead, celebrated Mass, and gave a decent burial to the criminal, however notorious.

The White Brethren also took care of the families of those who had been executed, especially families who were left in dire poverty. Every Saturday the members contributed towards a fund for this purpose, and eight of them, wearing their habits, would collect alms in the city for the welfare of widows and orphans.

Among those condemned to death, there were always some who were innocent and some who had been condemned for minor offences. Qualified members of the Confraternity worked strenuously for their release – and in this work of justice and mercy the legal skills of Alphonsus Liguori played an important part.

Deacon

Alphonsus was ordained a Deacon in 1726 and given permission to preach in all the churches of Naples – of which, at that time, there were at least five hundred. He preached his first sermon in a parish church celebrating the Forty Hours devotion. This devotion was celebrated in a different church each day. For many years Alphonsus had visited these churches every day and spent hours in prayer before the Blessed Sacrament exposed on the altar. Now he was in great demand to preach in the churches where this devotion was being held; and most of them were too small to hold the crowds that came to hear the famous ex-lawyer preaching.

With such a heavy workload – studies, preaching, confraternity commitments and severe personal penances – it was no wonder that he fell desperately ill and came close to dying. When the doctors had given up on him he asked for the statue of Our Lady to be brought to him from his favourite church – Our Lady of Ransom. No sooner was it placed at the foot of his bed than he began to recover. However, he had to convalesce for three months before he regained his former strength. Only then was he able to make ten days retreat in preparation for the priesthood.

Priest

Alphonsus Liguori was ordained priest on December 21, 1726, at the age of thirty. He has left no record of his feelings on that day, but from the resolutions he wrote we can gather the seriousness with which he viewed his vocation. Here are some of those resolutions:

- As a priest my dignity is greater than that of the angels – I must therefore be entirely pure and, as far as possible, an angelic man.

- At Mass God obeys my voice, and I must obey his voice, the inspirations he sends, and also the voice of my superiors.

- The Christian people look on me as a minister of reconciliation with God – therefore I must be always close to God's heart and never lose his friendship.

- Poor sinners are waiting for me to free them from the death of sin – I must do this through prayer, example, word and work.

- If I wish to please God, then recollection, intense desire, solid virtue, and the practice of prayer must occupy my time constantly.

As a young lawyer Alphonsus had drawn up a list of resolutions to ensure his absolute integrity in his profession. By adhering faithfully to those resolutions he had become the most outstanding lawyer in Naples. Now, as a priest, he would live out the resolutions he had made to ensure absolute fidelity to his vocation, and to the total commitment he had made to God. By fidelity to those resolutions during sixty years of priesthood he became one of the Church's greatest saints.

Preacher

For three years after his ordination Alphonsus remained at home at the request of his father. The two brothers next to him became priests, so he gave up his inheritance to his youngest brother, Hercules. For the first five years of his priesthood Alphonsus was in constant demand for missions, retreats, and special sermons. The chief characteristic of his preaching was its simplicity, its directness and its apostolic quality. What he said was clearly understood by rich and poor alike. This was totally different from the florid style of society preachers who dazzled their audiences with their turn of phrase, but conveyed no clear spiritual message. Alphonsus came over with conviction because he preached Christ crucified and not himself. He was accepted by everyone as a true apostle who sincerely practised what he preached. At the same time, with his warm, ardent personality he achieved instant rapport with his audiences. As a lawyer he had pleaded successfully for his clients. Now he was using his skills to win souls for God.

His father had shown no great interest in the work Alphonsus was doing, and was still bitter at the frustration of his plans. But one day as he passed the door of a church he heard Alphonsus preaching. Out of curiosity he went in to listen. He was deeply moved by the sermon. Impetuous as usual, he sought him out afterwards and embraced him. "O my son, how grateful I am to you!" he said. "You have taught me really to know God. I bless you and thank you a thousand times for embracing a state so holy and pleasing to God."

Confessor

As was the custom, Alphonsus did not receive faculties from the Bishop to hear confessions until one year after his ordination. Unfortunately at that time confessors were taught to take a hard line with their penitents, and not to give absolution easily. The idea was to safeguard the dignity and justice of God who had been offended. As a result people with grave sins were put off from going to confession, and even good people found it burdensome.

It was to be the great achievement of Alphonsus to change that attitude throughout the Church by stressing the mercy of God, and bringing sinners back to him through kindness and compassion. But, as a young priest trained in the school of severity, it was not easy for him to strike the right balance in the tribunal of confession. He was by nature scrupulous, having inherited that trait from his mother. And throughout his life he depended very much on the advice and guidance he received from his spiritual directors.

As a lawyer he could understand the textbook arguments for severity. But as a confessor, dealing with real people and real situations, he soon concluded that what was needed was not severity but the merciful compassion of Christ; and it was in that spirit that he dealt with his penitents. It was no wonder that his confessional was besieged by people of all degrees and every walk of life, seeking to make their peace with God, and to profit by the advice given them by a saint who understood.

Evening Chapels

When not engaged in missions or preaching in city churches, Alphonsus spent as much time as he could in the streets gathering the poorest people around him, instructing them in the faith, and bringing them closer to God. He would then lead them to the nearest church, prepare them for confession, and teach them some of his own hymns – which the people loved. He used all his talents in the service of God, and that included his gifts as a poet and a musician.

Out of this work, there grew a new movement which came to be called the Evening Chapels. Seeing his influence over the poor, other zealous priests and lay people joined him in the street apostolate. Soon it was possible to hold similar meetings at the same time in other parts of the city. Some of the people converted by Alphonsus to a better life were among his best trained group leaders; and they included teachers, tradesmen, barbers, and artisans of all description.

There would be rosary and prayers, instruction on the duties of the Christian life, and the method of making meditation. These meetings would last about an hour and a half. On Saturdays priests would hear confessions. On Sundays there would be meditation on the Passion of our Saviour followed by Mass at which all would receive Communion. Later in the day there would be a public visit to the Blessed Sacrament and to Our Lady for each group in their particular church. This Association of Chapels flourished for well over a hundred years.

All this work for those in special need was preparing Alphonsus for the task to which God was now calling him: nothing less than the founding of a new Religious Congregation whose main object would be to bring salvation to the most neglected and most abandoned souls.

The Chinese College

In June, 1729, Alphonsus finally left home, and together with his friend, the future Venerable Gennaro Sarnelli, took up residence in the Chinese College. This had been established by a former missionary to China, Father Matthew Ripa. At this time Alphonsus would have been quite happy to go to China as a missionary, especially as it offered the chance of martyrdom; but his spiritual director assured him that was not the will of God for him. While staying at the College, Alphonsus was given charge of the church and was responsible for its services. His preaching continued to attract large crowds, and he spent many hours in the confessional. His favourite reading was the lives of the saints, and he tried to emulate them in their zeal and penances. It was here that he took a vow never to waste a moment of time. It was here, too, that he met his future spiritual director, Father Thomas Falcoia, a close friend and director of Matthew Ripa. Father Falcoia had the makings of a saint but was an extremely authoritarian character who took charge of anyone who came within his orbit. His influence on Alphonsus would be immense.

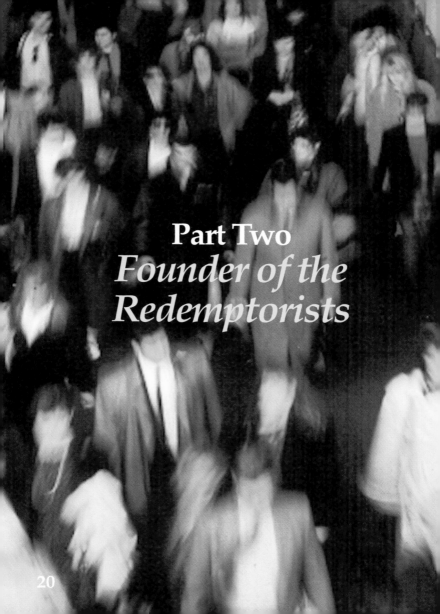

Part Two
Founder of the Redemptorists

After a particularly busy Mission in April, 1730, Alphonsus again collapsed from overwork. When he was sufficiently recovered, doctors insisted he should convalesce in Scala – a little town nestling high up in the mountains and facing the sea, some forty-three miles south-east of Naples. With a number of priest friends he set off in a carriage along the bumpy coast road to Amalfi. There they met the Bishop and were advised to climb up the mountain to a hermitage called Santa Maria dei Monti, overlooking Scala. This provided them with all the accommodation they needed, and had the advantage of a chapel next to it. The magnificent scenery and the view far out to sea was a tonic in itself; while the clean mountain air, and sea breezes soon made a new man of Alphonsus. What attracted him was the number of peasants, shepherds and goatherds in the area – all in desperate need of spiritual help. Here was a great opportunity for his missionary zeal. Holiday though it was meant to be, he would not be wasting a moment of time.

The Kingdom of Naples was certainly not short of clergy or religious. According to one estimate there were 138 bishops, 56,000 secular priests, 31,000 male religious, and 26,000 nuns. These figures may be exaggerated but they are not far from the truth. And yet, in spite of such numbers, the peasants in remote areas were completely neglected, with no one to care for their spiritual welfare. They knew scarcely anything about their faith and were spiritually abandoned.

Alphonsus and his companions immediately set about instructing these people, and preparing them for the sacraments. Word quickly spread, and shepherds, goatherds and peasants from miles around began converging on the chapel to receive the spiritual help so long denied them. After that experience Alphonsus knew exactly what his mission was to be – to found a religious congregation devoted entirely to the evangelisation and sanctification of the abandoned souls in the countryside.

Redemptoristines

Alphonsus returned to Scala in September, 1730, to preach the Novena in the Cathedral in preparation for the feast of the Holy Cross. After that he was due to give a retreat to a community of nuns in Scala. This convent was very much in the news, and events there had given rise to much controversy and ridicule in Naples. One of the Sisters, Maria Celeste, claimed to have had revelations from Our Lord, which made known a new Rule for the community. It was hard to know how much credence to give to her assertions. The spiritual director of the convent was Falcoia. As he had just been made Bishop of Castellamare, a neighbouring diocese, he was unable to visit Scala at that time. But he urged the Sisters to put all their problems to Alphonsus while he was preaching a retreat to them. The Bishop of Scala also left the whole matter to him.

After searching enquiries and much prayer, Alphonsus became convinced that the new Rule was truly inspired and could safely be adopted. Both the Bishop and Falcoia accepted the decision of Alphonsus, and on that basis the new Order of the Most Holy Saviour came into existence on Pentecost Sunday, 1731. On August 6, the feast of the Transfiguration, the Sisters were invested with their new habit. In future years they would be known as the Redemptoristines, and be closely associated with Redemptorist Fathers and Brothers in imitating the virtues of our Holy Redeemer, and sharing in his work for the salvation of souls.

A Call and a Decision

After all the excitement at Scala, Alphonsus was happy to return to Naples, to his missions and Evening Chapels. He did not forget the peasants he had met at Scala, and his desire to help them was as strong as ever. But the way forward at that point was not altogether clear. Perhaps God would give him a sign. He did not have long to wait. On October 3, 1731, Sister Maria Celeste received further revelations. This time they concerned the formation of an institute of men imitating the Saviour, and preaching the Gospel to the poor. In her vision Alphonsus was singled out as the leader of this new band of apostles.

When Alphonsus heard of this from Sister Celeste he was astounded and tried to play down the importance of the revelation, even though this seemed to be exactly what he wanted to do. He tried to excuse himself from the task by pleading all the work he was doing in Naples. But if it was the will of God how could he refuse to do it? On the other hand, who would join him in such an undertaking? His friend, Mazzini, with whom he was discussing the matter, offered to be the first of his companions, and assured Alphonsus more would follow.

During the following year Alphonsus made no move except to take advice from spiritual directors. He was strongly supported by Bishop Falcoia who was to be his principal director in all that concerned the future institute. But many opposed him, not least the Cardinal Archbishop of Naples who did not wish to lose such a tireless and saintly worker. Needless to say, his father, Giuseppe Liguori, put every obstacle in his way. His final tactic was a highly charged emotional one. For three hours he embraced and clung to Alphonsus, begging him with tears not to leave. Years later Alphonsus described this as the greatest trial of his life. But now he knew he had received a call from God, and he had made his decision. There could be no looking back – whatever the cost. During the first week of November, 1732, Alphonsus left Naples, riding on a donkey, and headed for Scala.

Redemptorists

The Congregation of the Most Holy Redeemer (C.Ss.R.) was inaugurated on 9 November, 1732, in a small chapel belonging to the Redemptoristines in Scala. In the presence of Bishop Falcoia, Alphonsus and five companions dedicated themselves to the imitation of Jesus Christ, and to the evangelisation of the poor. At the end of the Mass they all sang the *Te Deum* in thanksgiving. Later on, the inauguration was celebrated in the Cathedral amid great rejoicing by the people of Scala who were happy to know the Redemptorists would now be with them on a permanent basis.

This first Redemptorist Community was living in very cramped conditions, but rejoiced in all their hardships. They spent their days in study, silence, prayer and penance. They still had to work out the Rule by which they were to live, and this called for frequent discussion. It soon became clear that they all had different ideas, and each wanted his own ideas to be adopted. Some resented the authoritarian attitude of Falcoia who was determined to shape the new institute his way. Although he was the Founder, Alphonsus, in his humility, did not at this stage want to be anything more than an ordinary member of the Community. He was clear in his own mind that the only work for Redemptorists was to give Missions to the poor in the rural areas; however he consistently defended the authority of his spiritual director, Bishop Falcoia. He pointed out to the others the importance of having a Bishop at their head at least until they had the approval of the Holy See. Although another priest with long experience of Religious Life was appointed Superior of the Community, Falcoia would only deal with Alphonsus in all matters concerning the Institute. For his part, Alphonsus made it clear that it was up to him, as Founder, to establish or change the Rule, and to interpret it. There would be no going back on that.

The First Lay Brother

Only a few days after the Congregation was inaugurated the first lay brother arrived to complete the Redemptorist Community. By the age of twenty-six, Vitus Curzio had already had an interesting career. He admitted in his youth he had gone around with pistol and dagger. But more recently he had become respectable, and with a good education he had obtained the post of administrator of properties belonging to the Marquis of Vasto. In this capacity he had become a friend of Cesare Sportelli who was procurator general to the Marquis. One day he told Sportelli of a dream he had had. He was trying to climb a mountain with a number of priests, but kept falling back. Then one of the priests took his hand – and the rest was easy. Next day he and Sportelli happened to meet Alphonsus. "That was the priest who helped me climb the mountain" said Curzio. Sportelli told him Alphonsus was the famous preacher who was now founding a Congregation to work for the poor, and he himself was going to join him. Without further ado Curzio decided that must be his vocation also. Within a few days he had sold all he had and given the proceeds to the poor. When he arrived at the hospice in Scala he asked to join the Community as a lay brother. But when he was asked to serve at table he took it badly – after all, he was a gentleman. When Alphonsus got up from table to help him with the serving he felt thoroughly ashamed. From then on he became a pillar of support to Alphonsus and his faithful companion through the many trials that lay ahead. Curzio was the first of thousands of young men who have given their lives to God as Redemptorist Brothers and used their talents in the service of the Community and for the good of souls. Best known of all the Brothers is, of course, Gerard Majella, the patron saint of mothers. But many others, too, have reached great heights of holiness by fidelity to their vocation.

First Mission

Early in January, 1733, Alphonsus and his companions set out for the Tramonti district, a steep valley between mountains overlooking Nocera dei Pagani, with 12 villages and a total population of about 3,500. The missionaries took Vitus Curzio with them. Besides cooking for them in the house they rented, Vitus played a useful part in the mission, leading the prayers, giving catechism classes, and welcoming the people. The success of this first Redemptorist Mission led to requests for many more, and won the enthusiastic approval of the local Bishops. The joy of Alphonsus can be imagined now that he and his fellow Redemptorists were doing all he had dreamed of. When they returned home it was now to a house attached to the Cathedral. There, with the Bishop's permission, they established a perpetual mission with prayers and devotions, instructions and confraternities. To the delight of the Bishop, Scala soon became a holy city.

Desertions

Unfortunately, the first companions of Alphonsus could not reconcile their differences regarding the Rule, the purpose and way of life of the Institute they were trying to form. As a result three of them left to set up on their own in March 1733. This was a blow to Alphonsus, but he was already prepared for the worst, and had taken a vow to continue the work himself whatever happened.

New Recruits

He knew that if God wanted the Institute to flourish he would send new companions; and in this he was not disappointed. Within a few months he was joined by four new members who would remain loyal and be pillars of the Congregation. Like Alphonsus two of them had been lawyers, Cesare Sportelli and Januarius Sarnelli – both later declared Venerable by the Church. Another priest member was Xavier Rossi whose family made it possible for Alphonsus to make a new foundation at Villa in the diocese of Cajazzo.

Recruitment, however, remained slow, and was mostly confined to men already ordained priests. One of the conditions for ordination was that the priest must have an assured income to support himself, or belong to an approved Religious Order which would allow him to be ordained under the title of the Common Table. Sixteen years were to pass before the Redemptorist Rule was approved by Rome. And the new Congregation would not be approved by the King of Naples until after the death of Alphonsus. In the meantime, the State could put every possible obstacle in the way of Alphonsus. And many young men who offered themselves as candidates would leave because the life was too hard, or they were lured away by their families.

Foundations

Even the foundations he had made brought disappointments to Alphonsus. The house at Scala had to be given up because the town did not give the support it had promised, and local clergy claimed they were losing out because of the popularity of the Redemptorists. Villa had to be given up because of malicious gossip and a hate campaign conducted by a man whose partner in sin had been converted to a better life. The first foundation to last – not without problems – was at Ciorani in the diocese of Salerno. This was the gift of the Sarnelli family, providing for a church and a house big enough not only for a Community, but also for retreatants both clerical and lay. It was here that Redemptorists took their first religious vows and held their first Chapters.

Another foundation was made at Nocera Pagani in 1747. Although this was done at the request of the people, and made possible by the donation of one man's fortune, it provoked the usual hostility by jealous clergy and bitter anti-clericals. The King's permission had to be obtained before any religious house was built; and those who opposed the Pagani foundation did not hesitate to send letters to the King full of lies and false allegations. Alphonsus needed all his skills as a lawyer to counteract these accusations. In the end permission was granted. Pagani became the home of Alphonsus, and it was there that he died. Both Ciorani and Pagani continue as active Redemptorist Houses to this day.

Death of Falcoia

For some years before his death Falcoia had been in failing health. In 1742 he had a stroke. During his final illness he was assisted by Father Sportelli and Brother Francis Tartaglione. Almost his last words were a blessing on the Congregation, and a prophecy that it would grow and spread. He died on April 20, 1743. He had been a thoroughly dedicated priest and Bishop, and richly deserved the respect and reverence paid to him by Alphonsus. There had been times when Alphonsus had been close to despair under the weight of his trials. But Falcoia was always at hand to encourage him and restore his confidence. They disagreed over policy from time to time, and other members resented the way Falcoia used his authority to enforce his own ideas. Now that he was dead the time had come for the members to choose their own Rector Major. A Chapter was called at Ciorani for this purpose, and on the fourth ballot Alphonsus was chosen to hold this office for life.

Death of Giuseppe Liguori

In 1744 Giuseppe Liguori made a retreat at Ciorani. This so moved him that he asked Alphonsus to accept him as a lay brother. Alphonsus advised him to return home and edify all around him by a life of piety and virtue. The following year, while giving a Mission, Alphonsus received news that his father had died. He sent another priest to represent him at his father's funeral.

Another sad loss was the death of Vitus Curzio. He had been sent by Alphonsus to friends in Troia to seek help for the Community at Iliceto – a new foundation – as they had no food and no money. On the return journey he took ill and died. He was thirty-nine years old. Alphonsus wrote an account of his life, and singled him out as an example of what a lay brother should be.

Canonical Status

Following the death of Falcoia, the time had now come to put the Congregation on a sound footing after years of uncertainty. The approbation of both Pope and King would be needed. As a first essential step, the members took the Vows of Religion – Poverty, Chastity and Obedience – at the Chapter of 1743, adding an Oath of Perseverance. Because the State forbade the founding of new Religious Orders they described themselves as secular priests of the Congregation of the Holy Saviour, canonically established under the authority of the Ordinaries.

The Rule

The next step was to complete the Rule under which they lived. This had been a thorny problem and had led to many differences between Falcoia and Alphonsus. Now the Chapter empowered one man – most probably Alphonsus – to produce a complete Rule for all the members. This was a difficult task, and the final version did not appear until 1747, just in time to be approved by the Chapter convoked in that year at Ciorani.

Papal Approbation

Having tried without success to obtain the King's approval, Alphonsus decided to seek the approbation of the Pope, Benedict XIV. As it happened, the Pope's secretary was visiting Naples at the time, and offered to present the petition to the Pope personally. Several useful changes were made in the Rule as it was examined by Vatican officials. The Congregation was finally approved by Pope Benedict XIV on February 25, 1749, under the new title, Congregation of the Most Holy Redeemer.

This Rule was now accepted by the Chapter held at Ciorani in October, 1749. At the same time Alphonsus was re-elected as Rector Major.

Growth of the Congregation

The papal approbation gave a great boost to the Congregation, and vocations were now plentiful. By the year 1752 – twenty years after its foundation – the Congregation had 50 professed priests and students. Vocations came mostly through the missions. Thirty-nine missions were given in 1752, and thirty-two in 1753. Many of these missions lasted several weeks and transformed the morals of entire areas. The zeal and austerity of the missioners, and their powerful preaching made a deep impression. It was no wonder that young men with high ideals were drawn to the Congregation. Some who entered the Novitiate soon left because of the severity of the life – prayer, recollection, poor food and penance were the order of the day. Such a life designed to produce saints took a heavy toll, and many of the Congregation's most promising men died in their forties or even earlier. A good example of that was St. Gerard Majella, the miracle-working lay brother who died at the age of twenty-nine after only six years as a Redemptorist. Alphonsus shed tears at the death of these zealous members, but consoled himself in the knowledge that their prayers would now win even more graces for the Congregation and for the missions.

Foreign Missions

Ever since his days in the Chinese College, Alphonsus had burned with the desire to preach the Good News of the Gospel to those who had never heard it. Not only China was in his sights. He had heard, too, of abandoned souls among the people of South Africa. He would gladly have given up everything to bring the love of Jesus to all these people. Only the firm assurance that such was not the will of God for him, and his obedience to his spiritual directors, restrained him. However, in drawing up his Redemptorist Rule he made it clear that his spiritual sons must be ready to devote their lives to such missionary work when circumstances were right for it. This great wish of Alphonsus has now been fulfilled, and Redemptorists today are playing a significant part in mission fields throughout the world.

Writer

Alphonsus was well known in the Kingdom of Naples as a saintly missioner whose preaching had transformed entire regions. But as a writer – especially in the field of moral theology – his fame had quickly spread through the whole of Europe. He began serious writing after the age of fifty and produced a total of 111 books – he was one of the most prolific writers of the century. He began by writing for his novices and students, such works as "Visits to the Blessed Sacrament", and his "Moral Theology". But it was not long before these works had a wider readership. Translated into other European languages they went through many editions. With the trained mind of a brilliant lawyer, and the down-to-earth knowledge of innumerable penitents, he kept a well-balanced line between being too rigorous and too easy-going. When a law was doubtful he favoured freedom. His teaching met with much opposition, but in the end it prevailed throughout the Church. It is principally for this reason that he was declared a Doctor of the Church in 1871 and Patron of Confessors and Moralists in 1950.

Polemical Works

Alphonsus was well aware of the sorry state in which the Church found herself, not least in nominally Catholic countries such as France, Spain and Italy. Books undermining the faith of Catholics were to be found everywhere. Pornography and immorality abounded. There was virulent hostility to the Popes, and deep-seated anticlericalism. Atheistic writers such as Voltaire and Rousseau made vicious attacks upon the Church, and these were popular throughout Europe. In his "Moral Theology" he included two dissertations, one on "The Infallibility of the Pope", and one on "The Immaculate Conception of the Virgin Mary". Both of these doctrines he wished to see defined by the Church; and his support for them helped to pave the way for their definition in the following century.

With his ardent love of the Church it pained Alphonsus beyond measure to see the hurt and damage being inflicted on the faithful. He took up his pen to refute the prevalent errors, and into every book he wrote went months of research and long hours of writing. This had to be done between missions, retreats, and his duties as Rector Major. His nights were more given to prayer, study and writing than to sleep. On top of all this he kept up an enormous correspondence with priests and religious including all his own brethren in the Congregation. His health was always precarious, and he suffered greatly from asthma and arthritis.

Spiritual and Devotional Works

Alphonsus wrote more than sixty spiritual works, all of them down-to-earth and practical. His aim was to help people of all classes to love God, to pray, and to become mature Christians. There was nothing dry or merely academic about Alphonsus. He was always a true Neapolitan – ardent and affectionate by nature, and richly endowed with gifts of poetry, music and art. His love for God was nothing less than passionate; his devotion to Mary the Mother of Jesus always warm, childlike and affectionate. In his case, at least, religion without devotion would have been unthinkable. Devotion is the tender expression of the love for Jesus at the heart of the faith, and Mary and the Saints who exemplify it. Such devotion is a great support for the faith. By trying to eliminate the simple devotions of ordinary Catholics, the Jansenists had greatly reduced the rich quality of their faith. But in Alphonsus

Liguori the Church found a saint who would restore the spirit of true piety and devotion. Alphonsus was the complete antithesis of everything Jansenism stood for.

Among his devotional works still in use today are his "Visits to the Blessed Sacrament and to the Blessed Virgin", and "The Stations of the Cross". To these may be added some of our best known hymns: "O Bread of Heaven", "O Mother blest", "Look down, O Mother Mary".

By his preaching, his missions and his personal sanctity, Alphonsus won many thousands of souls for God, and stemmed the tide of Jansenism, materialism and unbelief. By his writings he has been a shining light in the Church for the past 250 years. In declaring him a Doctor of the Church in 1871, Pope Pius IX did not hesitate to say: "Alphonsus, by his learned writings and especially his 'Moral Theology', dissipated and destroyed the darkness of error resulting from Jansenism and unbelief."

"Let us love Jesus and Mary
and become saints.
We cannot hope or pray
for anything better.
Farewell then, until we meet
in paradise, at the feet of this
most sweet Mother and of
this most loving Son.
May we praise them there
and love them face to face
for all eternity. Amen."

St. Alphonsus Liguori
Introduction to the Glories of Mary

Part Three
The Bishop

Bishop Liguori

At a time when he could have been justly excused if he had retired from public life, especially in view of his broken health, Alphonsus was suddenly commanded by Pope Clement XIII to accept the bishopric of St. Agatha of the Goths. Several times earlier he had narrowly escaped episcopal honours; but now, in 1747, when he was 65 years old, there was to be no escape. All appeals failed. The Pope was inflexible. Alphonsus was completely broken by the news, and could not disguise his feelings. However, to Rome he went, and there was consecrated bishop. For the next thirteen years he put into practice all he had written in his book: "Reflections for Bishops". He was distinguished by his zeal, his apostolic simplicity, his love of the poor, and his hatred of all outward show. At the same time he remained Rector Major of the Redemptorists and ruled the Congregation through his Vicar, Father Villani.

St. Agatha of the Goths

This was one of the 131 dioceses in the Kingdom of Naples. It had a population of about 35,000, served by 300 diocesan priests, with 13 monasteries. In spite of such a number of clergy it was not possible for Alphonsus to provide priests for the abandoned people in the rural areas. These people were too poor to build their own churches and could not afford to support a priest of their own. In any case, few of the priests would be willing to leave their homes and the local neighbourhood for which they had been recruited.

The Clergy

There was, of course, a minority of priests who were well-educated and took their duties seriously. But the majority, as in the rest of the Kingdom, were poorly trained, theologically ignorant, and totally lacking in pastoral commitment. Many had entered the priesthood with the sole object of obtaining a lucrative benefice with only light duties, a good income, and, because of their clerical state, freedom from taxation.

Many took secular employment, but most lived with their families and spent much of their time drinking and gambling. Some who held high positions in the Church gave scandal by living in concubinage and parading their children on the streets. Previous Bishops had kept a blind eye to these scandals and the deficiencies of the clergy. That was not to be the style of Bishop Liguori, and he lost no time in warning the clergy that scandals would not be tolerated, even if it meant offending some of the most powerful families in the diocese.

He also made it clear that benefices would only be given on a basis of merit. When he arrived at St. Agatha's he found the rooms in the palace full of presents from the wealthy and the powerful. Every gift was returned to its donor with a word of thanks from the Bishop, and a clear statement that it was against his principles to receive any gift. In this way he would keep himself free from outside influence in the important decisions he would have to make. He had a mandate from the Holy See to reform the diocese, and nothing would deflect him from this purpose.

The People

With the clergy setting so poor an example it was no wonder morality was at a low ebb among the people. As they were rarely instructed they knew very little about their faith. They lived largely on a diet of devotions which could easily deteriorate into superstition. Promiscuity was widespread. Couples intending to marry lived together with the approval of their parents. Alphonsus was well-informed about the situation, and had his plans ready to deal with it. At his enthronement in the cathedral he announced a mission for the whole diocese, beginning at St. Agatha's the following Sunday.

The Mission

Alphonsus himself led the Mission and started off with a rousing sermon on Hell. At the end of the sermon he put a curse on all who were living in concubinage if they refused to reform their lives. His threats were no empty words. As the law stood in the

Kingdom of Naples, adultery and prostitution were crimes to be punished with whipping, imprisonment and banishment. Alphonsus did all in his power by gentle persuasion to reform the delinquents. But when all other means failed he handed them over to the civil courts and allowed the law to take its course. Rich families were outraged when some of their high-ranking clerical members were arrested and put into gaol. Their appeals to the King fell on deaf ears. The Ministers of Justice gave Alphonsus their complete support. The diocese soon got the message that the new bishop meant business, and reform was not slow to follow.

Results

The Mission spread to the whole of the diocese during the following year. Alphonsus attended as many Missions as he could, and preached not only to the people but also to the clergy. They were told in no uncertain terms how they had to run their parishes, with daily Mass, morning prayer, and public visits to the Blessed Sacrament and Our Lady every evening. On top of that the priests had to attend weekly meetings for theology courses and the study of rubrics. This was indeed a Mission with tangible results, and a lesson for the other 130 dioceses in the Kingdom of Naples.

Father of the Poor

Both as a Redemptorist and a Bishop Alphonsus showed great love and compassion for the poor. When presented with a list of fees connected with his consecration in Rome he refused to pay them. "I did not ask for the episcopacy; it was imposed on me. The only way I have of paying these charges is out of the revenues of my church, and these revenues I must use in relieving the poor." The Pope, Clement XIII, ordered the fees to be waived in the case of Alphonsus, and remarked, "When Monsignor Liguori dies there will be one more saint in Heaven".

When he arrived at St. Agatha he found an expensive banquet had been prepared to welcome him. Alphonsus expressed his dismay and scolded his secretary: "Do you think I have come here to give banquets when so many of the poor are in need? Let nobody want for anything at my table, but there must be nothing superfluous". As far as possible he continued to live as he had done in the monastery, choosing for himself the poorest room, keeping up all his austerities, and imposing an order of the day on his household which included morning and night prayers even for his guests – no matter how important they might be.

Nevertheless, the poor were always welcome, and did not have to stand on ceremony to approach him. He was accessible to all who were in real need, and he gave alms liberally. Every evening he visited the sick and the house-bound before going to the cathedral for the public visit to the Blessed Sacrament. The Canons of the Chapter had difficulty in preventing the Bishop from selling the treasures of the cathedral to give more to the poor. However, when a disastrous famine hit the Kingdom of Naples in 1763, it was to Bishop Liguori that the poor of the diocese turned in their extremity. And he did not fail them.

The Great Famine, 1763-64

For at least two years before it happened, Alphonsus prophesied that a great famine was imminent. In 1761, while preaching in Naples against the vices of the capital, he said: "Take care, you who live only for the pleasures of the senses. God will punish you with famine". Preaching in his cathedral in 1762 he warned the people: "Next year the dearth will begin its ravages. People will be driven to eat grass to survive". Whatever the signs, neither the people nor the authorities did anything about it.

In November 1763 the famine began. The crops had failed and there were few reserves. During the first six months of 1764 more than 300,000 people died of starvation in the Kingdom of Naples. Rich people bought and hoarded whatever grain was still available, hoping for still higher prices when they sold. Bakers had no wheat to make bread. Vegetables were scarce and expensive. As Alphonsus had prophesied, the poor were driven to eat grass and herbs to survive.

Believing in his own prophecy, Alphonsus had bought large quantities of beans, peas and dried vegetables, filling all the Palace store rooms months before the famine began. People wondered if he had gone crazy. However, they were happy enough to take their share of the Bishop's bounty once their own foodstocks were exhausted. Hundreds of people came every day to the Bishop's Palace looking for food, and no one was turned away. When the people rioted against the local Council, blaming them for the shortages, the Mayor fled to the Palace for his own safety. Alphonsus faced the raging mob and invited them to kill him instead of the Mayor. He then doled out whatever was left in his supplies, and the people returned home in a quieter mood.

Alphonsus was now at his wits end how to find more supplies as the winter dragged on. He sold everything he could lay his hands on – a few pieces of jewellery, his rings, his pectoral cross, and even his carriage and mules. In his book, "Reflections for Bishops", he had written: "The Bishop must understand that the Church does not provide him with an income to spend it on what he wishes, but to aid the poor". As a result of his charity and organisational ability thousands of his people were saved from death by starvation.

Resignation

By 1775 Alphonsus had been Bishop of St. Agatha of the Goths for thirteen years. During that time he had effectively reformed the diocese; brought the clergy into line with the requirements of the council of Trent; provided them with the basics of moral and pastoral theology; insisted upon correct rubrics at Mass; dealt firmly with scandals and abuses; re-organised the seminary and ordained only those he deemed worthy. At the same time he had written several books and brought out new editions of his famous "Moral Theology". Now, in his seventy-ninth year, he was finally permitted to resign his see by Pope Pius VI, on account of his accumulated infirmities which had left him paralysed and crippled. His head was painfully bent upon his chest. For two years it had been impossible for him to say Mass; and now he could say it only with the greatest difficulty, sitting down and aided by two assistants.

The sorrow of his people in losing their beloved pastor was very much in evidence. None grieved more than the working mothers to whom the Bishop had been a friend indeed. To enable them to go to work he had turned his own residence into a daycare centre where mothers could leave their young children. At his own expense he arranged for the children to be well-looked after and well fed. Such care was virtually unknown in those days. No wonder those mothers lamented his departure, realising that the daycare centre would not survive. Their sorrow was probably more heartfelt than that of the clergy who knew their Bishop as a loving father, but also a strict disciplinarian.

However heavy the Bishop's heart on leaving his Diocese, there was still room for joy and relief when he arrived at the Redemptorist house at Nocera Pagani. Here he was given a royal welcome, and a solemn *Te Deum* was sung in the church to celebrate his return. "It is like being in Paradise," he said, so happy to be back among his religious brethren. Sitting at the piano which he had not played for thirteen years, he remarked: "Now that I am no longer a bishop I may take a little recreation.'" Unfortunately, he found himself unable to play, as his head was so bent down that he could not see the music. However, he laughingly agreed to compose some fresh music, something really good for his funeral, which he assured them would be very soon. As a matter of fact he still had another twelve years to live, and they were to bring him the greatest sorrow of his life.

For the first few years of his retirement he insisted on keeping up all the spiritual exercises of the Community, and often preached in church. His favourite subjects were the love of God, the importance of prayer, and devotion to Our Lady. Far from being idle, Alphonsus got through a prodigious amount of work. People of every rank from all over Italy came to discuss their problems and to seek his advice and prayers. For the first two years he was able to continue writing. Considering his huge literary output for the benefit of the church, Pope Pius VII wished to possess as relics the three fingers of the right hand with which Alphonsus had written his works. He might have made a fortune from his books, but as he was writing for God and the people he refused to accept one penny from the profits. Needless to say, his publisher, Remondini, was a life-long friend.

Betrayal

For a man of his advanced years, utterly broken in health and living in constant pain, Alphonsus showed immense vitality. But as age and sickness weakened him still more, he had to rely increasingly upon his Vicar and Consultors in all that concerned his Congregation. He became stone-deaf and almost completely blind. He lived more and more within himself, leading a deeply spiritual life, and leaving external affairs to others. It was the supreme tragedy of his life that in this dark hour he was betrayed by the men he trusted, and all his work for the Congregation undone by them.

There were at this time four Redemptorist houses in the Kingdom of Naples, four in the Papal States, and one in Sicily. Although the Redemptorist Rule had been approved by Pope Benedict XIV, the King of Naples had refused to ratify it. Without such ratification the Institute could have no legal status in Naples. If Alphonsus had allowed the regalist Ministers of State to alter the Rule according to their own ideas, approbation could have been obtained at any time. But it was precisely to preserve the Rule that Alphonsus had held out so long, and endured so much persecution.

Then, in 1779, when Alphonsus was 83, there seemed a chance of getting the royal approbation, as the Minister responsible was himself a Religious, and appeared to be favourably disposed. Unable to handle the matter himself, Alphonsus deputed two Fathers to act in his name. They soon found, however, that the Minister was a complete regalist, and had no intention of allowing anything to remain in the Rule that was opposed to his Government's policy. He slashed the Rule mercilessly, cutting out the three vows, taking away the authority of the Rector Major, and making no provision for General Chapters. Furthermore, the delegates were given an absolute command to adopt the revised Rule under pain of suppression. On these conditions the royal approbation would be graciously given. Only one thing was now required to put these changes into effect, and that was the signature of Alphonsus.

While these negotiations were in progress, news of what was happening began to leak out, and Alphonsus was inundated with letters of protest from indignant Fathers. But the Saint simply refused to believe such tales, and went on trusting his treacherous representatives, accepting their repeated assurances that all was going well. In the end, when they came for his signature, his eyes were too weak for him to read the document, and he signed it on the assurance of his Vicar that no substantial change had been made.

When eventually an official copy of the new Rule was sent to him, Alphonsus realised that he had been tricked into signing away all that was most dear to him. The aged Saint shed bitter tears, and for a long time was unable to speak. A group of Fathers stood around him and tried to comfort him. At length, when words were possible, he reproached and condemned himself without mercy. "I ought to be dragged through the streets," he said. "It was my duty as Rector Major to read the manuscript myself. But you know," he added pathetically, "I find it difficult to read even a few lines." Then turning to his Vicar he said to him: "Don Andrew, I never thought I could be deceived in such a way by you. I have been betrayed".

Only those with a clear understanding of the political background in Naples at the time can understand the hopeless situation in which the negotiators had found themselves. Their dilemma had been a very real one. Either to accept the Rule enforced by the Government, or to be suppressed and disbanded. They chose the former course, hoping the primitive Rule might still be observed in practice, and fully determined that it should be. They knew Alphonsus would never agree to this procedure, so they kept him in the dark, hoping that things would come right in the end. Meanwhile they felt the best service they could render the Congregation was to keep themselves together, to continue their work, and preserve their houses intact.

In the end, things did come right. Providence used this catastrophe as a means to propagate the Congregation far beyond the confines of the Kingdom of Naples. This was exactly what Alphonsus prophesied when he had recovered his calmness after the storm now breaking around him.

Expulsion

The Redemptorists in the Papal States refused to accept the new Rule and appealed to the Pope. When Pius VI heard of this latest example of State interference in Naples, he was in no mood to listen to explanations. With his supreme authority he declared that only the houses in the Papal States would be regarded as belonging to the Congregation of the Most Holy Redeemer, and that all those in Naples were excluded from membership.

The news of this heavy sentence and of the Pope's wrath were made known to Alphonsus as he was preparing to attend Mass. He broke into tears, and began accusing himself of ruining the Congregation through his sins. After a while he gained control of himself, and said with great calmness: "I will only what God wills. His grace is sufficient for me. The Pope will have it so. God be praised". During the day, however, the misery of the whole thing broke upon him with shattering force, and he cried out for help: "O my brothers, help me!" The Fathers led him to his room and comforted him as though he were a child. After several hours the storm abated, and he was able to say: "O my Mother Mary, I thank you, for you have supported me. Help me, O my Mother".

Scruples

And so, under the shadow of the Pope's displeasure, the valiant defender of the Papacy came to the end of his long and holy life. For five more weary years he lingered on, being purified in great suffering, as is often the way with God's saints. As though his cup of bitterness was not already full, Alphonsus was now subjected to every sort of temptation, and tormented by scruples. The only thing that saved him from losing his mind altogether was his obedience to his confessor. He who was the prince of Moral Theologians and the friend of all poor sinners was made the special target for attack by the powers of Hell who had good cause to be angry with him.

Joy for the Future

In 1785, two years before his death, news reached Alphonsus that two young Germans had been admitted into the Noviciate in the Redemptorist House in Rome. This filled him with the greatest joy, and he did not hesitate to prophesy: "These two Germans can accomplish much good as priests. God will not fail to spread his glory through these men into those lands which have been partly abandoned since the suppression of the Jesuits." One of those German recruits was St. Clement Mary Hofbauer, the Redemptorist saint who was to establish the Congregation in Northern Europe. Now, 200 years after the death of St. Alphonsus, Redemptorist missionaries are continuing his work of evangelisation in Europe, Africa, North and South America, Australia and the Far East. Alphonsus can rest content: his dreams fulfilled, his sufferings rewarded.

Death

It was fitting that when the end came in his ninety-first year, Our Lady should answer the prayer so often addressed to her by Alphonsus: "I implore thee, O Mary, to meet my soul when it is about to leave this world, to comfort it by thy presence, and to receive it into thy hands!" Those present at his deathbed were all convinced that Our Lady appeared to him, so completely transformed was his face, so lit up with a heavenly smile, as he gazed for the last time upon a favourite picture of the Madonna. He died in great peace, surrounded by his brethren, upon whom he had bestowed his last blessing. His blessed soul went to God as the church bells were ringing the Angelus on the 1st August, 1787.

A vast number of people came to pay their last respects to the venerated remains of the holy Bishop and Founder. To permit an even greater multitude to join in this last act of homage, the church authorities arranged to carry the body in procession to the neighbouring village of Nocera and back again. But the peasants of Pagani were not prepared to trust their neighbours in Nocera, and were quite sure they would never see the body again. So they made such an uproar that the procession had to be called off. Alphonsus would probably have enjoyed that touch, so typical of the simple people he had loved and served for so many years.

Reunification of Redemptorists

We can surely believe that Saint Alphonsus prayed powerfully for the healing of the rift in his Congregation caused by the action of the Neapolitan Government. Within four years of his death the Government had changed its policy and ordered Religious to revert to the Rule under which they had first been professed. This made possible the reunification of Redemptorists in the Neapolitan Kingdom and in the Papal States. This took place at a Chapter held in 1793 at which Father Paul Blasucci was elected Rector Major. At that time the Congregation counted 180 Fathers and Students, a large number of Brothers, and 17 Houses. From then on the Congregation continued to grow until it became one of the largest Religious Congregations in the Church.

Honours

The Pope who had come down so heavily on the Neapolitan houses after the change of Rule, had never ceased to be a warm admirer of Alphonsus personally. He was angry, however, that advantage had been taken of the Founder's incapacity to introduce changes which the Holy See would never countenance. His personal regard for Alphonsus was clearly shown when he waived aside many of the initial processes, and allowed the cause for his beatification to be introduced at a very early date after his death. Miracles were not wanting in testimony of his heroic sanctity; his reputation was world-wide. The only possible objection arose from his apparent acceptance of the new Rule imposed by the Neapolitan Government. A commission of Cardinals was appointed to examine the whole question, and they unanimously agreed that there was no stain whatsoever on his character. The Pope accepted this verdict, and the cause proceeded. Alphonsus was beatified in 1816 and canonised in 1839. His feast is now celebrated on 1 August.

St Alphonsus was declared a Doctor of the Church in 1871. Celebrating the centenary of this declaration, the Archbishop of Venice, Albino Luciani, later to be Pope John Paul I, singled out the life of Alphonsus as a mirror in which his clergy could measure their life and ministry. He mentioned the Saint's sense of humour, his love of God and concern for the poor, his devotion to the Blessed Sacrament and the Virgin Mary, his missionary zeal and style of preaching, his care of priests and seminarians, his careful use of time and his profound theology.

Pope John Paul II highlights the place of Alphonsus in history: "St. Alphonsus is a gigantic figure, not only in the history of the Church, but for the whole of humanity as well. Even people who would not seem close to him in the sense of having followed his vision, still see in him the teacher of the Catholic souls of the West. He did for modern Catholicism that which St. Augustine accomplished in ancient times."

For further reading

Alphonsus de Liguori –The Saint of Bourbon Naples 1696–1787
Frederick M. Jones, C.SS.R.
Gill & MacMillan, Dublin

St. Alphonsus Liguori –Tireless Worker for the Most Abandoned
Theodule Rey-Mermet, C.SS.R.
New City Press, New York

Appendix I
St Alphonsus Liguori: A Chronology

1696	Born at Marianella, near Naples
1708	Entered University of Naples
1710	Became local Councillor by privilege
1718	Doctor of Canon and Civil Law
1723	Called to the Priesthood
1726	Ordained Priest
1731	Co-founder of the Redemptoristines
1732	Founder of the Redemptorists
1736	Established foundation at Ciorani
1749	Redemptorist Rule approved by Pope Benedict XIV
1762	Consecrated Bishop of St Agatha of the Goths
1763	Severe famine
1775	Resigned as Bishop; returned to Redemptorist house at Pagani
1780	New 'Royal Rule' rejected by Rome
1781	Alphonsus and Neapolitan Redemptorists excluded from Congregation by Pope Pius VI
1787	Death of Alphonsus
1793	Redemptorists re-united under original Rule
1816	Alphonsus beatified
1839	Alphonsus canonised
1871	Declared a Doctor of the Church by Pope Leo XIII
1950	Declared Patron of Confessors and Moralists by Pope Pius XII

Some notable persons mentioned in this life of St Alphonsus

Maria Celeste Crostarosa (1696-1755), born in Naples in the same year as Alphonsus, was a Carmelite nun in Scala where Thomas Falcoia became her spiritual director. She received visions of our Lord expressing his wish for the founding of two Institutes based on a close imitation of Christ, the most holy Redeemer. Like Alphonsus, she was for a time excluded from her Order, and had to leave the community at Scala. She wrote several spiritual works and the Rule for the new Order. Maria Celeste died in 1755 and was declared Venerable in 1901.

Thomas Falcoia (1663-1743), joined his friend Matthew Ripa, who returned from China and founded the Chinese College. Alphonsus met Falcoia there and chose him as his spiritual director. He became deeply involved in the establishment of the Redemptoristines and the Redemptorists. Although a dominating personality, his faith in both institutes made him a great support and encouragement to Alphonsus in difficult times.

Gerard Majella (1726-1755), joined the Redemptorists as a Brother after attending a Mission in his village. He was, at first, turned away because of ill health, but became proficient in everything to which he turned his hand. He was renowned for his life of prayer, for the wisdom of his counselling and advice, and he was much sought after to assist on parish Missions. He became known as a wonder-worker and is invoked in a special way as patron saint of mothers and mothers-to-be. He was canonised in 1904.

Clement Hofbauer (1751-1820), was born in what is now the Czeck Republic and became a Redemptorist in 1784, the first from outside Italy. Sent to Vienna to establish the Redemptorists north of the Alps, his zeal took him to Warsaw where he began the famous "perpetual mission". His work destroyed when Napoleon captured Warsaw in 1808, Clement returned to Vienna, where he had an enormous influence on the life of the university. His inspiration helped the spread of the Redemptorists across Europe and to America. Clement was canonised in 1909 and declared Patron of Vienna by Pope Pius X in 1914.

Cornelius Jansen (1585-1638), professor of Theology at Louvain and specialist on St Augustine, he became Bishop of Ypres in 1635. After the posthumous publication of his book *Augustinus* his teaching spread through the Chuch – human nature was a slave of sin, grace was given only to the elect few and the sign of election was a spirit of fear. Jansenism was extremely rigorous and exercised a very damaging and negative influence in the Church for centuries. Alphonsus was implacably opposed to its teachings.